Capricorn

The determined goat
typifies the sign
of Capricorn.

Capricorn

22 DECEMBER TO 20 JANUARY

Your Guide to Health,
Wealth and Success

Contents

About this Book

 f you know your Sun sign, read your horoscope in the newspaper for fun or perhaps wonder if there really is anything in the stars, then this *Pocket Astrology* is your friendly guide. If your birthday is between 22 December and 20 January your Sun sign is Capricorn and this book is for you.

Find out how your Sun sign can influence every aspect of your life, from what you wear to who you are likely to fall in love with, how you cope with family life and what your dream job might be. Discover the power of your ruling planet, the nature of your opposite sign and why Venus is so important in your birth chart.

The goat has many of the qualities of Capricorn.

There is a *Pocket Astrology* volume for each of the twelve Sun signs, which makes it easy to understand how the heavens influence your friends and family, too.

It's All in the Stars

 strology, as we know it in the West, was developed over 4000 years ago by the ancient Babylonians and Chaldeans in what is now modern Iraq. At that time there was no difference between astronomy and astrology. The ancient stargazers noted that the Moon and the planets all appeared to move across the sky on the same broad pathway and that in the daytime the Sun travelled along the centre of this path as it apparently orbited the Earth.

Astrologers in ancient Babylon were the first to follow the movements of the Sun, Moon and planets.

It was not until 1543, when the Polish astronomer Copernicus (1473–1543) established that the Sun, not the Earth,

An astrolabe was used to measure the altitudes of the stars.

is the centre of our universe, that this was explained. The Earth and the other planets orbit the Sun in roughly the same plane, and consequently always appear in the same band of sky. The constellations (groups of stars which appear to make a pattern from a viewpoint on Earth) that form the backdrop to this movement were first used as a reference grid, a convenient way to pinpoint planetary positions. Eventually, twelve such constellations were noted and they began to assume special personalities of their own, collecting their own myths and attributes. They were also given names, mostly of animals. That is

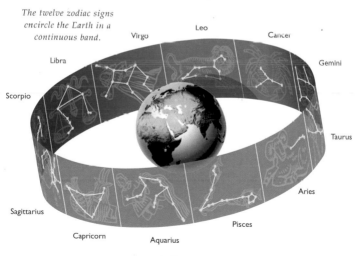

The twelve zodiac signs encircle the Earth in a continuous band.

Leo

Virgo

Cancer

Libra

Gemini

Scorpio

Taurus

Sagittarius

Aries

Capricorn

Pisces

Aquarius

why this band of sky is called the zodiac, from the Greek word for animal.

The zodiac signs in Western astrology have the same names as the constellations

Earth is the element that influences Capricorn.

but, due to the gravitational effect of the Sun and the Moon on the Earth over a long period of time, the signs and constellations no longer coincide. There are twelve zodiac signs and the Sun appears to take a year to pass through them all, spending roughly a month in each one. Capricorn is the tenth sign. There are other special aspects to your Sun sign. Each has a quality, an element and a gender. There are the three qualities:

Powerful Saturn is your ruling planet.

SATURN AND CAPRICORN

Saturn is the planetary ruler of Capricorn. It is the sixth planet from the Sun and best known for its stunning rings. Before more distant planets were discovered, Saturn was considered to patrol the outer limit of the known universe. It spends about 2½ years in each zodiac sign.

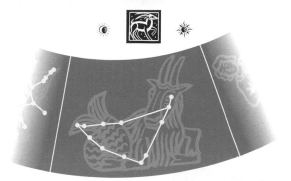

The image of the goat is formed by the constellation of Capricorn.

The Capricorn Myth

The constellation Capricorn is represented by the goat. Traditionally, this was Amalthea, the she-goat that suckled baby Zeus when his mother hid him from the wrath of his father. Amalthea brings a generosity of spirit and a love of humanity to Capricorn.

Cardinal (enterprising, initiating), Fixed (resistant, constant) and Mutable (adaptable, changeable); the four elements: Fire, Earth, Air and Water; and the two genders: feminine and masculine, which are more like the Eastern concept of yin and yang than any biological definition. These concepts form a mathematical pattern round the zodiac so that no sign has exactly the same configuration as another. Capricorn is a cardinal, feminine, earth sign. Each sign is also ruled by a heavenly body. Capricorn is ruled by Saturn, who was named after Cronos, the father of Zeus.

The Capricorn Personality

he symbol of Capricorn is the goat, the tough little animal that thrives in harsh terrain and does not regard a mere mountain as an obstacle. As a Capricorn, you are a determined individual who will work steadily to attain your goal, however long it may take. Your careful and considered attitude to everything in life is a legacy from your stern planetary ruler, Saturn, the planet that teaches us to learn from our experiences. This rather forbidding influence means that career success may come at the middle or end of your working life – but it will come. You need to feel appreciated for

Goats know what they want and work hard to achieve it.

Capricorns achieve goals in middle age or at the end of their working lives.

Loyal and pragmatic,
Capricorn likes to feel
appreciated.

KEY TRAITS

* hard-working
* determined
* reliable
* ambitious
* sensible
* loyal
* stubborn
* controlling
* pessimistic
* moody
* mean

*Friends and family enjoy
your wicked sense of humour.*

all your hard work, otherwise your self-esteem may plummet and your nimble hooves lose their footing. Most of the time, however, you are quite outgoing, appear self-confident and have a wickedly acerbic sense of humour. Respect, status and security (physical, spiritual and financial) are essential to Capricorn well-being.

To the rest of the zodiac, Capricorn may seem chilly and stand-offish, especially at first meeting. This is often the result of genuine shyness and inhibition but there may be a regrettable tendency to treat people as things and to go for politic friendships and trophy partners.

Cronyism is a very Capricorn concept. Nonetheless, loyal and dependable, competent and funny, Capricorns are much loved by those who can get past the sometimes forbidding exterior. However, friends and family might secretly wish that you did not moan quite so much about your lot in life and that you tried to regard change as an energizing principle rather than an enemy to be avoided at all costs.

Your polar opposite sign is the sign that faces yours across the circle of the zodiac. The polar opposite to Capricorn is Cancer. Polar opposites have a strong bond, although they

Emotional Cancer is Capricorn's polar opposite.

may find relationships difficult. They always share the same quality and gender – in your case, feminine and fixed – but different elemental energies; you are an Earth sign, Cancer is a Water sign. Both are keen to help others make sense of the world, but express themselves in different ways. Capricorns offer practical, pragmatic help; Cancer offers comfort and sympathy for the spirit.

Capricorn Health

ost Capricorns are hardy and can thrive in the kind of bleak conditions that may be too severe for other members of the zodiac. They have plenty of wiry strength and stamina but need to work on mobility and flexibility of body, mind and spirit. Of all the signs, Capricorn is the most likely to become a workaholic. Capricorns should consciously build in leisure time to their agenda to defuse stress, which may cause stomach problems.

CAPRICORN CRYSTALS

Crystals are considered to vibrate with healing energy.
Each zodiac sign and ruling planet also has its own energy.
These are Capricorn's crystals.

Onyx:
to strengthen
bones.

Malachite:
to reduce
stress.

Howlite:
to cheer
the spirit.

Tigereye:
for happy
independence.

The celebrated Capricorn self-discipline means that few members of this sign let themselves get out of shape. If they think they are piling on the pounds or getting a little flabby, they will take themselves in hand. A sensible, balanced diet is needed to sustain Capricorns through their long hours of hard work.

The ever-reliable potato provides you with the energy you need.

Self-motivated and well-disciplined, Capricorns do not need a personal trainer to goad them into exercise. They simply set themselves a programme and follow it.

Jogging or a regular workout at the gym will keep you fit. Serious fell walking and rock-climbing may also appeal. The goat's capricious element means that most Capricorns are very fond of dancing. Some may make it their career – they have the stamina and determination to put in the necessary hours of practice.

Each sign rules a particular part of

You have no problem with the self-discipline needed to keep to an exercise regime.

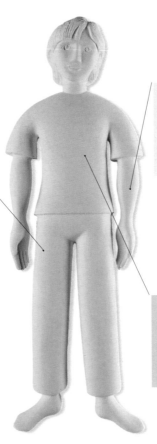

**CAPRICORN
RULES
THE BONES**

Keep up your
calcium intake to
strengthen bones
and teeth.

**SATURN RULES
THE SKIN**

You may be prone
to minor skin
irritations.

*Your Sun sign,
your polar
opposite sign
and your
ruling planet
all influence
your health.*

**CANCER RULES
THE BREAST
AND LUNGS**

Stress may show
itself in breathing
difficulties.

You have the stamina to enjoy running over rough terrain.

the body and each planet also has its special influence. The polar opposite sign is also considered to be very significant in health matters. This means that you may be vulnerable in the parts of the body ruled by Capricorn, Cancer and Saturn. Protect them as much as possible, and be aware that any stress in your life may show itself in those areas. Capricorn rules the bones, teeth and knees, Cancer the breast, chest and stomach, and Saturn the skin, skeletal system and spleen. Be prepared for possible aching bones, toothache, stress-induced stomach problems and minor skin problems.

Thyme is particularly good for treating rheumatism and aching joints.

Capricorn Style

The keynote to Capricorn style is elegant quality. Capricorns are often blessed with good bone structure (Capricorn rules the bones), and clothes hang well on you. You tend to choose the functional and practical over the stylish and frivolous, although this does not mean you will not insist that clothes are well designed and properly made, preferably from natural fabrics. Both male and female Capricorns understand the power of a well-cut suit. Whatever Capricorns are doing, they

Good quality shoes are important to Capricorn.

ACCESSORIES

* **custom-made shoes**
* **practical hat**
* **good quality briefcase or handbag**
* **discreet jewellery**

generally like their dress to be appropriate for their current activity and prefer to change clothes when they change activity, rather than go through the whole day in the same outfit.

Capricorn's accessories are as grown up as their wardrobes: good quality briefcases or

Dark earthy green and navy blue are some of Capricorn's colours.

handbags and handmade shoes if they are very rich. The overall look is businesslike. Capricorns also seem to like hats.

Capricorn's colours draw on a rather wintry palette: black, grey, brown and navy, enlivened with earthy colours such as rust and olive green. Colours from your polar opposite sign may also attract you: these are blue and silver, the Cancerian colours with the shimmer of the sea. Many Capricorns have a weakness for a subtle sheen on the fabrics of their immaculately cut clothes.

You look good in smart, formal styles.

Capricorn Wealth

 apricorn coffers may only occasionally overflow but they are never empty. Most Capricorns are successful at making money, but not sensationally or overnight. Whatever their income, they are generally able to budget extremely efficiently and get a lot out of a little. On the whole, Capricorns are generous to their family and loved ones, and will often help out relatives in financial distress. However, the restrictive influence of your ruler, Saturn, makes you careful with your cash and sometimes this may be seen as meanness. Of all the zodiac signs, Capricorn will probably be

Dark sapphire

You are careful with money and keep your accounts up to date.

Garnets

Rich, dark blues and reds are the colours of Capricorn's gemstones.

the one most familiar with the pros and cons of the many complicated deals on offer from banks, building societies and financial institutions. Most of them keep immaculate books recording income and expenditure and are likely to know the precise state of their finances down to the last penny. Even young goats keep track of their pocket money. The rough and tumble of the stockmarket is often too exhilarating for Capricorns. They are unlikely to speculate, unless it is with a set amount of money they can afford to lose. Even then, they will choose with care and caution where they invest. It can be fun (and profitable) to choose businesses or industries with a Capricorn slant: banking, agriculture, pension funds, big business of any kind and the silver market are all sound Capricorn choices.

THE CAPRICORN METAL

The Capricorn metal is lead. This is solid and useful rather than beautiful and Capricorns could swap it for pewter or silver for decorative purposes.

JUPITER RETURNS

Every 12 years, the planet Jupiter returns to the exact place it occupied in the heavens at the moment of your birth. Jupiter is the planet of expansion, joy and good fortune, and these should be propitious times for you.

Most Capricorns have a very strong material streak. They are ambitious to succeed in their particular world and very concerned about status and its visible signs. Outlay on the home and garden, a well-engineered car, smart personal appearance and education will be considered money well spent. One common Capricorn indulgence is really good whisky and some keep a modest cellar of single malts. That said, your spending habits are not normally lavish. You prefer to invest in quality, comfort and good value. If Capricorns have accounts stuffed with cash, they will probably spend substantial amounts on complicated high-yielding pension schemes.

Capricorns with money like to spend it on obvious status symbols like a fast car and good whisky.

Capricorns tend to go for classic, discreet jewellery.

Of course, wealth does not simply mean cash. According to astrological lore, each sign has its own precious stones. The Capricorn gemstones are dark sapphires, garnets, moonstone and white onyx. Although it is not a gemstone, jet is also very suitable for Capricorn.

Capricorn jewellery is usually of the discreet kind made by established and reputable houses. The design is likely to be conventional, unless it is an expensive, avant-garde piece that signals the wearer's status in the world. As they know that time is money, Capricorns of either sex usually tend to wear elegant, precision-engineered watches.

Capricorn at Work

apricorns take work really seriously. Whatever the task, they bring their full attention to it. Honest, dutiful and dependable, Capricorns are very adept at spotting the main chance and grabbing it to help them up the ladder to status and success. They like tradition and routine, distrust innovation or lateral thinking, and need to feel they are in charge of the situation. For Capricorn, doing it their way is the only option. They may appear to have an exaggerated sense of their importance in the team and insist on petty formalities. This is often because they are quite insecure inside and

Many Capricorns love the real-life monopoly of the property market.

Cézanne, a Capricorn, was not only a famous artist but also a banker.

need to bolster their self-esteem. Capricorns do well in careers that make the most of their methodical administration skills and give them adequate scope for rising through the ranks.

Suitable Capricorn career choices might be: bank worker, accountant, property manager, estate agent, gardener, farmer, osteopath, dentist, administrator in any kind of big business, publisher, politician.

Whatever the job, you like to be in control of your particular section of it and need to work with people who respect your methods but who can temper your rather inflexible approach and tease you into revealing your wicked humour on appropriate occasions. Fellow cardinal signs

Capricorns are often drawn to politics and many will aim for the top job.

Cancer and Libra can do this, and flirtatious, mutable Gemini brings out the lighter side of Capricorn. Piscean disorganization and the more slapdash side of Sagittarius make these signs less suitable for Capricorn to work with. Fixed-sign people (Taurus, Leo, Scorpio, Aquarius) are your equals in grit and determination. All is well if you all agree on procedure. If you don't, business will come to a standstill, as compromise is the hardest word for any of you to say.

BEST CAPRICORN JOB

Capricorn's ideal job offers them responsibility, autonomy and status. It must be in a serious business and close to the smell of money. In an ideal world, Capricorn would be the manager of a pension fund, with all the perks that go with that position.

The Capricorn working method is equally suited

An established bureaucracy with everyone in their place suits Capricorn well.

to large organizations and self-made businesses. Putting a system in place, applying tried-and-tested methods, and networking in all the right places all form part of the ambitious Capricorn's strategy for success and can be applied in any work situation. Most Capricorns like a formal working environment with due respect for rank and title. They need to be appreciated, respected and rewarded for the work they do, and hate to be passed over for promotion or forced to change their established working practices. Be aware that your austere and autocratic attitude and rather forbidding manners can drive away more light-hearted members of the zodiac.

A working relationship with Gemini is good for both signs

SATURN RETURNS

Saturn returns to its original position in your birth chart every 29½ years. It is the planet of limitation or consolidation. These are the times when you say goodbye to your wildest dreams and settle for reality. By accepting the limitations of your situation at these times, you are able to plan for the future.

Capricorn at Play

any Capricorns find it almost impossible to fit any fun into their lives. Indeed, some very ambitious goats only play to promote their interest at work: a politic round of golf with the company chairman or a corporate entertainment at the opera or the racetrack. Very few Capricorns idle their leisure hours away lolling on a sofa. However, they should learn to take time off, as all work and no play makes Jack a dull boy. Even then, Capricorns who do have hobbies tend to work just as hard at them as they

Capricorns often enjoy going to concerts or the ballet.

Capricorns love a challenge – however daring!

do at their jobs. You are likely to spend your time off with your nose buried in a good book or working industriously on an item of craftwork. Many adore quizzes and quiz shows and, naturally, know all the answers.

Active pursuits with a hint of competition and challenge are usually favoured: for example, hiking in the country, preferably over fairly rough terrain on a predetermined route. Capricorns like the idea of completing a certain walk, or climbing all the peaks in a range of hills. Gardening is usually a major hobby, with green-fingered Capricorn

> **HOBBIES**
>
> * reading
> * dancing
> * hiking
> * gardening
> * playing and listening to music

tending the plants and assembling the
immaculate potting shed. And they
are very fond of golf, even if not
playing with the boss.
Although they may
find leisure hours
difficult to build
into their
agenda, most

*Top golfer
Tiger
Woods is a
competitive
Capricorn.*

*You take pride in your
garden, which you keep
in very good shape.*

Capricorns will insist on their
right to a fixed holiday or two
in the working year. No
Capricorn would just pick up a
passport and go. Everything
will be planned and budgeted
down to the last detail. Many
Capricorns choose holidays
with built-in educational
value: lectures, guided trips
around ancient sites, free
entry to museums.
Mountain resorts are

GRAND PASSION

Music liberates the conservative Capricorn soul. Listening to, performing or writing it transforms many Capricorns. Others express themselves through dance, especially formal disciplines such as ballet or ballroom dancing, where there are rules and a ladder of achievement to climb.

usually very popular, especially if they are near lakes. As Capricorns are often uncomfortable in the heat,

Many Capricorns like dancing.

winter holidays are a good choice and you would probably enjoy making progress on the ski slopes.

Your opposite sign may have some influence on the way you spend your leisure hours. Cancer may encourage a penchant for collecting antiques (they are good investments as well as reminders of the past) and for cooking (especially bread and cakes).

Capricorn in Love

he position of the planet Venus in your birth chart has a great influence on your love life. If you don't recognize this portrait of Capricorn in love, it may be because Venus, the planet of love, was in a less cool and collected sign when you were born. To find out where Venus was at the time of your birth, and what this means in the context of your birth chart, you need to consult an astrologer.

Aloof, self-contained and rather shy, Capricorns often find it difficult to make contact with the opposite sex and

LOVE AND MARRIAGE

Good partners for romance
Gemini, Aries, Leo.
♥ ♥ ♥ ♥ ♥

Good partners for marriage
Fellow Capricorns, Taurus, Scorpio, Pisces, Virgo.

Classical and traditional: Capricorn's romantic gesture will be a dozen red roses.

can appear uncaring. This is because they fear rejection and the dizzy freefall of love. They hate being unable to control a situation but once they are sure of their ground they reveal their delightful flirtatious side and can become generous lovers. Do not expect public demonstrations of passion; Capricorns prefer a dignified and grown-up attitude. This does not mean they are prudes, simply that they regard love and sex as private matters.

Marriage is a very satisfactory institution to Capricorn. It rationalizes romance, confers status and provides security. Most Capricorns have no problem remaining faithful once they have made the commitment, and enjoy family life. There is a strong urge to fulfil traditional stereotypes: the male Capricorn likes to be seen to be in charge of the

Marriage and commitment suit Capricorn well.

relationship, the female will often appear to be content to be the good woman behind the great man.

Capricorn, Family and Friends

apricorns are usually very keen on traditional
family values. In their eyes, family comes first,
and this means extended family and in-laws as
well as the immediate unit. You tend to be proud, loving
parents but find it difficult to express your affection
physically and may impose your own goals on children

who do not share your vision.
Children from a Capricorn
home will emerge hard-
working, trustworthy and
either reticent or rebellious.

*You can become rather self-
important, especially in meetings.*

CAPRICORN IN SOCIETY

Serious, grown-up people
(whatever their age), Capricorns
are often pillars of society.
Cautious and conventional, they
are not about to break the
rules, although they can be
contrary and recalcitrant when
the rules do not suit them.

*Family life
and traditions
are important
to Capricorns.*

Young Capricorns in the family are usually conscientious,
loyal and honest. However, they can be rather shy and
tend to take themselves rather too seriously.

Capricorns make dependable friends, and are
probably content with one or two good friends rather
than a constellation of acquaintances. Make sure you do
not miss their wonderful dry remarks and witty jokes,
which often emerge when you least expect them.

Capricorn gets on best with: Taurus, Virgo, Scorpio
and Pisces; finds it harder with Cancer, Aries and Libra;
and enjoys stormy relationships with air-propelled
Gemini and fiery Leo. Relations with the neighbouring
signs, Sagittarius and Aquarius, are usually cordial.

Capricorn at Home

 A pleasant and comfortable home is very important to most Capricorns, who like to find a refuge when they get back from a hard day's work plus overtime. Inside the house, Capricorns go for conventional style, with elegant furniture (a few antiques if they can afford them) and a rather masculine feel: natural fabrics and leather upholstery, perhaps, and the minimum of knick-knackery.

The Capricorn home often features masculine colours and textures.

In general, Capricorns like a glimpse of grass, and so might prefer country living, but what they want most is their own patch of territory and a wide view all around.

Capricorns are generous hosts as long as you don't upset their routine by dropping in unexpectedly.

An alpine rock garden is ideal for Capricorn.

Dark shades and natural materials find favour with Capricorn.

When invited, you will be offered traditional good food and excellent drink in a rather formal setting, but Capricorn's choice of music will make the occasion an enjoyable experience. If they can relax enough to lower their guard, Capricorns can be great company.

A garden of some kind is essential to Capricorn. As many Capricorns choose to live high up, this may be just a window box or balcony but it could be a roof garden.

Most Capricorns are fond of animals; indeed they are often able to express affection for their pets much better than they can for their human companions. They admire the self-containment of cats and warm to a family dog (after all, it is also a burglar alarm).

A friendly labrador will be welcome in Capricorn's home.

Your Capricorn Child

apricorn babies seem rather aloof and shy
and may be resistant to cuddles. However,
they have gorgeous, beaming smiles, all the
more precious for their rare appearance and they
hardly ever indulge in attention-seeking
performances worthy of Oscar nominations. If a
Capricorn baby is crying, there is always a reason.
They need a routine, and get fretful if it is
disrupted. Capricorn babies
approach everything slowly
and cautiously, but progress
steadily with walking and
talking. Show them books as
early as you can; they will
probably be early readers.

*Encourage
enquiry
with a junior
chemistry set.*

*Capricorn
babies like
toys that are
easily sorted.*

To keep the Capricorn baby
happy, offer activity toys
appropriate for his or her
age: books, puzzle toys, a
baby gym. Older children

may like a toy calculator, a play post office, a junior chemistry set or a musical instrument. Little girl Capricorns may demand, and really love, ballet lessons.

When your young Capricorns get to school, they will seem a little shy at first but will soon enjoy themselves. They like discipline and structure and will work hard and steadily to get as near to the top of the class as they can. They are usually popular both with teachers and their peers, and are successes on the sports field. Make sure their early education includes plenty of music and reading. To keep Capricorn children happy, remember that they tend to be loners. Do not force them into company but make sure they have some social contact. Encourage them to relax and enjoy their leisure time and try to josh them out of grumbling.

Young Capricorns overcome their shyness when they are comfortable with family and friends.

Taking Things Further

his book has given you an idea of your Sun-sign profile, but this is just a broad-brush picture. There are many other astrological factors to be taken into account to produce an individual portrait: the position of the *Moon* and the other planets and their relationships with each other; the identity of your *Ascendant* and your *Midheaven*; and where the *signs* and planets align with the astrological *houses* in your birth chart.

You can draw up your own birth chart; and there are books that offer step-by-step instructions.

Your birth chart is a map of the heavens as they were arranged at the moment you were born. To produce an accurate chart, you must know exactly what time you were born and where. However, it is the interpretation of the raw data drawn up in the chart that is important.

A qualified astrologer can interpret the meaning of this data with reference to your personal profile. This is best done on a one-to-one basis with a reputable astrologer. You can contact the Faculty of Astrological Studies or the Association of Professional Astrologers for a list of consultants.

Your astrological profile is influenced by the position of the *Moon*, which represents your inner self. The *Ascendant* is the zodiac sign that appeared on the eastern horizon at your birth – this influences your personality. *Midheaven* is the point in the sky that was exactly overhead at the same moment: this represents the expression of your individuality and your aspirations. An astrologer will pay particular attention to any *aspects*; these are precise geometrical relationships between the planets on your chart. Aspects can be powerful, moderate or weak and their significance is interpreted according to their proximity to planets, signs and houses.

A professional astrologer will interpret your birth chart to build up a picture of your personality.

This is an example of a birth chart drawn up by a qualified astrologer.

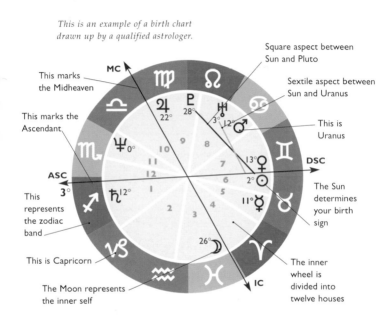

This marks the Midheaven

This marks the Ascendant

Square aspect between Sun and Pluto

Sextile aspect between Sun and Uranus

This is Uranus

The Sun determines your birth sign

This represents the zodiac band

This is Capricorn

The Moon represents the inner self

The inner wheel is divided into twelve houses

KEY TO SUN SIGNS

♈ Aries	♋ Cancer	♎ Libra	♑ Capricorn
♉ Taurus	♌ Leo	♏ Scorpio	♒ Aquarius
♊ Gemini	♍ Virgo	♐ Sagittarius	♓ Pisces

THE TWELVE HOUSES

The inner circle of the birth chart is divided into twelve houses which relate to the aspects of your daily life. Capricorn rules the tenth house; any planets in the tenth house will have a strong influence on your career and place in society.

1 The **first house** concerns itself with how you perceive the world and are perceived by it.

2 The **second house** represents your values, resources and capabilities.

3 The **third house** is the hub of communication and the expression of your mind.

4 The **fourth house** shows how your home and family life nurtures you.

5 The **fifth house** expresses love, creativity and children.

6 The **sixth house** organizes your work and health.

7 The **seventh house** harmonizes your relationships and marriage.

8 The **eighth house** deals with joint business and finance, sex and death.

9 The **ninth house** expands your life through philosophy and religion.

10 The **tenth house** promotes your career and social status.

11 The **eleventh house** indicates your friends and ideals.

12 The **twelfth house** is your desire for service to others, escapism and spirituality.

* * * *

This is just an introduction to what is a wide and fascinating subject. If you would like more information, then please contact the following:

The Association of Professional Astrologers
80 High Street
Wargrave
RG10 8DE

The Faculty of Astrological Studies
54 High Street
Orpington
Kent BR6 0JQ